Growing Dank Weed

A Simple Guide to Producing
Top-Grade Marijuana

© 2016 Elias van Rijn

Hello & Welcome!

You are about to learn how to grow your own delicious weed.
Growing marijuana seems and could be complicated If you don't
have the right information and advice. Too many people out there
make it seem that you need a degree in weed to be a grower. That's
why I have made an effort to make this guide easy-to-follow and
wrote in plain English. I do not believe there's any value in going
through books that are filled with hundreds of pages of fluff looking
for gems.

I have been growing weed for 13 years now and I've invested a lot
of time into educating myself along the way. I sifted through a lot of
info and have figured what works the hard way. Now you're about
to gain from my experience and knowledge. This book is geared
toward intermediate and new growers. I will give you the exact step
by step you need to follow so you produce outstanding bud and I'll
try to cover any question you might have.

Growing your own weed is actually easy and anyone with few spare
minutes a day can do it. It is also an extremely fun and rewarding
experience. Back when I began taking this hobby of mine seriously, I
remember reading somewhere that marijuana is in fact not
addictive, but you could get hooked on growing it. Of course I
laughed off this idea at the time, but now 13 years down the road, I
could admit that I do enjoy more growing weed than smoking it on
a regular basis.

Playing with that magical plant is very fulfilling in itself and then there are the extra benefits of not having to pay shady dealers silly amounts of money for bud that was produced god knows how. Commercial growers out there are concerned with one main thing: big yields. And they do take shortcuts to get there. There's nothing like blazing and enjoying self-produced top notch quality bud knowing that is as pure and natural as they come... and all that being **essentially free**.

Once you spark the fruits of our own labor for the first time, you truly appreciate the time and effort that went into that. Cannabis is a very resilient plant too, so even if you don't do a perfect job growing it, the results are still going to match or beat the quality of commercially grown bud. They call it weed of a reason - practically it grows on its own, given that you provide it with what it needs:

- Growing medium - **soil** is by far the easiest and most secure choice
- **Light** - either sunlight or grow lights of the right spectrum
- The right amounts of **nutrients**
- **Air** - well ventilated grow area
- Pure **water**

Let me thank you and congratulate you on taking the first step in this fun journey! If there is anything that you need help with, go to the concluding chapter of the book to get my email address; **do not hesitate to shoot me a message and I will be happy to help!**

Happy growing!!

Table of Contents

The Basics - If You Are Completely New to Growing

• Cannabis is strong, fast growing plant. It literally grows like a weed, that's why it is easy to grow.

• Cannabis plants can be male or female. To produce smokeable marijuana, only the female plants are being used. Males are being removed.

• Marijuana plants has 2 phases: Growth (or **vegetative**) and **Flowering** phase.

• During growth, the plant builds up its scaffolding of branches and leaves. It tries to grow as fast as possible. In nature, this happens during spring until midsummer.

• During flowering, most of the plant's energy goes into producing buds. The growth of new stems and leaves will slow down.

• The plant knows when to switch from growth to flowering by the light duration and light color.

• In spring and early summer, the days get progressively longer. The light is more blue. Once the longest day of the year has passed, the days are slowly getting shorter again. And the sunlight turns more red. Now the plant knows that it is time to grow buds.

• Under artificial lights, we start young plants under 18 hours of light and 6 hours darkness. At this time, we use lamps that are more blue in color. The plant 'thinks' that it is spring and grows as fast as it can.

• After 3-4 weeks, we change the light duration to 12 hours on / off and swap the light bulbs to something a bit more red. When we do that the plant starts flowering.

• Under artificial light it will take around 4 months for a plant to go from seed to harvest.

• Cannabis is a hungry plant. Fertilizer must be given in regular intervals.

• Medical marijuana and 'regular' marijuana are the same thing.

• Marijuana seeds can be bought online

Let's Get to Know Cannabis Just a Bit Better

Cannabis or hemp is one of earliest domesticated crops. It was used in China for textile production more than 6000 years ago. The same plant has been documented as being used in India for medicinal purposes for at least 4000 years.

Just as humans, cannabis plants have genders - male and female. On average, 5 out of 10 **regular** (non feminized) seeds will turn out to be male and 5 female. When the plants reach maturity, the male flowers produce pollen which fertilizes the female flowers in order to produce seeds. Male plants are no good for our purposes and we are only interested in the female plants. The female flower is what we call a bud and it produces sticky resins which act as glue for the male pollen. If a female gets pollinated it will stop producing resins and that's why we remove the males before they spoil our crop - we want our buds to get as sticky as possible, because that's where the magic is.

These resins contain *tetrahydrocannabinolic* compounds which are responsible both for the high and the medicinal effects. There are at least 60 different *cannabinoids* known so far. Tetrahydrocannabinol (**THC**) and cannabidiol (**CBD**) are the most important ones. THC is psychoactive - that is the secret ingredient that gets you high. CBD on the other hand is non-psychoactive, but it has therapeutic and medicinal benefits. THC and CBD go hand in hand and you could not have one without the other, but you could have different ratios between the two according to the strain. This is important if you are mostly after the medicinal properties of marijuana even though research on CBD is still in its infancy.

There are two main types of cannabis plants - **Indica** and **Sativa**. In reality, **most strains are hybrids** - a mix between Indica and Sativa.

Indica - think *RELAXED, STONED, COUCH LOCK*
They are short and produce dense resinous buds with a pungent smell. The smoke varies in taste, but it is heavy and it tends to make you cough. Smoke too much and you will be glued to the couch. They take less time to finish than to Sativas.

Indica and indica dominant strains usually contain higher **CBD** amounts.

Sativa - think *ENERGETIC, HIGH, CLEAR HEADED*
They grow tall and produce fruity smelling airy buds. The smoke is light and fruity. It gets you energetic and creative, sometimes making you feel like a kid that wants to play. Sativas take longer time to finish.

Sativa and sativa-dominant strains usually contain lower **CBD** amounts.

THC content will vary according to the particular strain, regardless if it is dominantly Indica or dominantly Sativa. **Lower THC** to **higher CBD** content ratio produces a more lethargic high. **Higher THC** to **lower CBD** content ratio will produce a more energetic high.

Depending on your **preference** or **condition** you will want to go with a Sativa or Indica strain with the according THC to CBD **ratio**. Most people prefer a nice balanced high, mild body stone with nice cerebral effects.

All cannabis strains have two growing phases - **vegetative** (growth) and **flowering** (budding). In both Indica and Sativa these are influenced by the amount of uninterrupted light they receive per day - the **photoperiod**. Outdoors in nature, marijuana will be growing during late spring and summer while the length of each day is longer than the night. In fall, when the days begin to be shorter than the nights they will start flowering.

When growing indoors, we emulate nature by exposing our plants to longer periods of light during the vegetative phase - e.g. a cycle of 16 hours of light and 8 hours of darkness - and 12 hours of light and 12 hours of darkness during flowering.

Many novice growers are asking how much will a certain strain yield. The answer is always tricky because of the photoperiod. It is hard to estimate how much you will yield, because the longer you keep your plants vegetating, the bigger they will get and so will be the size of the harvest.

There is a third variety of cannabis called **Ruderalis**. Ruderalis is "auto-flowering", which means that flowering is not triggered by the photoperiod. They start to flower automatically when they reach a certain age - roughly 2 to 3 weeks. They take around 3 months from seed to finish. Generally, serious growers avoid autos as they are considered to produce subpar quality, but there are also advantages such as multiple harvests in one season due to the short life span.

I will guide you through selecting the right variety of marijuana for you. Before moving on to that, let's consider the growing environment.

Should I Grow Indoors or Outdoors?

If you are not sure already, that's the very first question to ask yourself. If you live in a city you probably don't have too much choice and you will want to grow indoors. However, if you have options when it comes to the growing location it might be worth exploring them as plants love **sun** more than anything.

Outdoors

Outdoors your plants will need much less babysitting as they are in their natural environment. Sunlight and fresh air are abundant, so these are not your responsibility. Your yields will be significantly larger - a single plant could easily yield anything from a pound (half a kilo) up to ten pounds (when you become good at this). Plus, **outdoors the overall costs are next to nothing**. If people in your area grow tomatoes outdoors, then the climate is also great for marijuana! On the downside, privacy could be a concern and it is possible that your plants get pollinated naturally by wild pollen carried by the wind which will produce some seeds.

If you live in a non-prohibition state my best recommendation is to grow in a greenhouse, if that's an option for you, so you can have the best of both worlds - free light and protection from unpredictable factors.

Indoors

Indoors you can discretely produce a year-round supply of weed, but **the costs are significantly higher**. You will have to mimic nature and create a thriving environment for your babies. You have full control over the growing environment, so you could produce weed of consistent quality over time. *This is great*, but it is also a bigger responsibility as you are in charge of <u>everything</u> that your plants need - light, temperature, humidity, nutrients, etc. Depending on your level of enthusiasm, in the beginning this could seem overwhelming for the first time grower, especially in the beginning when you tend to overthink everything.

Genetics - Choose The Strain That's Right for You

Seeds

You can order seeds online, please choose a supplier from my List of Reputable Seed Banks. There are indoor and outdoor strains available. Healthy seeds are hard like nuts and beautifully marble colored. Dead seeds are hollow or totally black. You can store seeds in an airtight container in a fridge for 2 years.

Feminized seeds

Fem seeds produce only female plants. This is achieved by forcing a mature female plant to self-pollinate itself by stressing it. The offsprings carry only female genes so all of them are female as well. This is completely safe and paying the additional premium for feminized seeds is well worth it.

Genetics

First and foremost, **working with good genetics is the most critical aspect of your grow**. Even the most experienced grower in the world will grow shitty quality weed if he starts with shitty seeds. Therefore, choosing a reputable source for your seeds is critical. At the end of this chapter, I have compiled for you a list of seed banks that are known for quality and they deliver to the US. A lot of seed banks don't. Make sure to stick to the list as there are lot of scammy websites out there trying to sell you low quality beans. Please don't use bag seeds as the likelihood of wasting your time, effort and money on growing them is huge **even if the weed that they came out of was really good.**

For the lucky few growers that live in non-prohibition states, getting solid genetics strains is usually easy. Most dispensaries will happily sell you seeds and clones of strains that you have actually tried and like.

You might want to research laws in your area regarding possessing cannabis seeds. However, it should be noted that no one in the US has ever been arrested for having ordered seeds from the internet.

Choosing Your Strain

Don't just pick a strain based on what's hot at the moment i.e. Girl Scout Cookies or strains that are simply popular. 99% of popular strains are not the best choice for your personal stash. They are popular mostly because of their high yields and good potency. You should consider two factors when choosing your strain - the growing environment and your personal preference.

Personal preferences

Typically, if a strain is doing well in the yield department, it usually is not as potent or it might not finish as quickly as you may like. Fortunately, there are lots of strains that meet a healthy balance of all important considerations.

How strong do you like your bud? Some people have potency as their highest priority due their tolerance that's built up over time. Others may prefer a "functional high" with more pronounced qualities such as flavor and aroma. Do you prefer dank funky bud or the softer fruitier types? Are you going for a relaxing "narcotic" high (indica) or are you after more for an energetic "trippy" high (sativa)?

Addressing these questions is a good starting point... and you may even discover half of the fun is growing different varieties to find your very favorite. There are all sorts of different highs, bouquets and aromas to be experienced, just like foods and beverages.

Practical Considerations

If you have the fortune of not being limited by space and/or security concerns, then strains that get bigger and produce optimal yields would be an attractive option. However, if you must keep your grow discrete and/or you are going to grow indoor in a limited space, more compact plants may be the wiser choice.

How to Choose a Medical Strain

Most patients haven't grown or even tried cannabis before discovering it as medicine. Also strains are good for recreational purposes are not always suitable for specific medical conditions.

As a rule of thumb, strains with higher CBD to THC ratio is what patients are after. CBD content of 1% and above is considered high. More and more new strains with high CBD content of even 7% are coming to the market. These allow patients to experience the benefits of medicinal cannabis without experiencing a strong psychoactive effect.

Assessing the condition and symptoms you seek to relieve is the best starting point. Furthermore, the subjective experience of using marijuana is different from person to person, so the only way to discover what works for you is to experiment with different strains and hybrids with different indica/sativa ratios.

List of Reputable Seed Banks

The following seed banks are known throughout the 420 community to offer some of the best quality seeds and available out there:

https://www.nirvanashop.com/en/?idev_id=3440
http://www.seedsman.com/en/cannabis-seeds
http://www.sensibleseeds.com/
https://www.seedboutique.com/catalog/
http://2fast4buds.com/
http://www.midweeksong.com/
https://www.gorilla-cannabis-seeds.co.uk/
https://www.discreetseeds.co.uk/
https://www.cannabis-seeds-bank.co.uk/
http://www.zamnesia.com/35-cannabis-seeds
https://www.royalqueenseeds.com/

Avoid These Beginners' Mistakes

There's a learning curve to just about every activity, and growing marijuana is no different. People who have been growing weed for 20 years are naturally going to be a lot better at it than those who have just decided to start. But, most newbies might be dissuaded from trying it because they fear failure. These are some of the common mistakes that novice growers should avoid.

Keep it Private

Don't talk to anyone about it. Growing herb is a private endeavor that should be conducted in a "need to know" basis. I know how hard it gets when you have so much enthusiasm built up, but just don't discuss growing marijuana with anyone. The number one reason people get caught is snitching. Once the grower shares their secret, it can open a Pandora's Box of unnecessary drama. Talking about growing marijuana is a no go. Keep it to yourself. Better safe than sorry.

Poor Genetics

Planting unknown seeds will bring unknown results. While it may be a fun experiment to grow a few seeds from a particularly tasty bud, it's best to know exactly what one is investing their time, energy, and resources into. Seeds from reputable suppliers will always produce better results. The end product is weighted heavily in favor of the plants genes over the growing conditions, so by starting with proven seeds you will vastly increase you chance of some high quality plants and a decent yield.

Touch/Kill Danger

It's best to start the seeds in their growing medium as opposed to sprouting them with paper towels that will require moving the tender seedlings into their medium.

Timing the Growth Cycle

Sowing the seeds in late May or the first week of June provides the plants the perfect amount of time to complete their growing cycle in the least amount of time while producing the maximum harvest. After the summer solstice, days start becoming shorter. This induces the plants to move into their flowering and budding stages without unnecessary excessive height growth. Indoor growing environments should mimic this example.

Growing Culture

Cannabis plants are arid drought-resistant plants that require good air circulation, good drainage and suffer from too much water and food. In outdoor situations, sandy loam soil is optimal. They should be watered when the top two to three inches of soil are dry.

Overwatering

The other aspect to avoid is overwatering your plants, which can actually happen if your plants are growing in containers that are too large for them. Beginner growers tend to water a container until all the soil is damp, which usually ends up being too much water for their little roots to absorb. The water will sit in the pot, depriving your plants' roots of valuable oxygen, and this can lead to the symptoms of overwatering. Overwatering can also occur when a new grower is watering their plants too often. You will notice the symptoms of overwatering when the plants droop, but luckily it's fairly easy to fix, and it usually doesn't kill off the plants... although it certainly is capable of doing that, when left unchecked. The key is always to press your finger into the top inch of your soil to make sure that it is dry. If it isn't, don't water yet. If it is dry, however, it is the perfect time to quench your plants' thirst. Don't neglect to test it this way every time, or you could end up with the serious symptoms of overwatering.

Feeding The Plants

It is very common for new growers to give their plants far too many nutrients than what is necessary. They have the mindset that you can never have too much. That, unfortunately, is not true. Part of the issue is that store-bought plant nutrients include a feeding schedule. New, naive growers try to follow that schedule, but it almost always instructs you to feed your plants far too high doses of nutrients.

Organically grown cannabis plants taste and burn better, but time-released fertilizer is acceptable. Start with a 25% dilution and gradually increase the potency of the food. If the leaves curl or show other signs of malformation, flood the plants and spray the leaves with water.

Harvesting Too Early

Whilst the anticipation of your first grow will no doubt be overwhelming, playing the long game will reap much larger buds. As a general rule of thumb wait until the plants have stopped growing and the white pistils are somewhere between 50-70% darkened. Resist the temptation to harvest the plant until the pistils are mostly brown. Hang the plants upside down in a dark room with good air circulation until the stems are completely dry, then pick the buds, and begin the curing process.

Keep The Pesky Officers Out

If the room you grow in has a window visible to anyone from the outside you will need a solid curtain to block any light leaking out. You will be having your grow lights on for 18 to 24h a day during the vegetative phase. Police officers have an eye for these things... so it won't be too long before they start suspecting that something illicit is going on, if the lights are visible from the outside every night. Having a blackout curtain will also help during the flowering period as it ensures that no sunlight will leak in disrupting the flowering cycle.

Also, as you know, buds tend to have a funky smell. Cannabis plants give off that same distinctive smell while growing as well, especially towards the end. The scent could make neighbors or unexpected visitors such as the delivery man suspicious if it leaks out your grow room. You must make sure that your window is well closed.

Window growing won't cut it most of the time. Despite the fact that the best source of light for any plant is the sun, growing them indoors and using the window as your only light source is a bad way to go. Marijuana plants need as much light as you can give them. While it might be cheaper to just try to use the sun, it won't be effective. Buy lights if you're growing indoors.

Be prepared. Growing marijuana comes with a lot of vagaries that can leave you feeling overwhelmed. There are also plenty of things that you should just be prepared for. The plants need water, nutrients, light, and CO_2 (not exactly in that order). But, plants can also be hit with a bug infestation, lack of nutrient quality, and inadequate amounts of CO_2. Make sure you have a contingency plan ready in the event that the plants start to exhibit negative signs.

Be active. As you might have already guessed, growing marijuana is not a passive expenditure of your time. These plants need to be cared for almost like they are your children (however ridiculous that might sound). They have remarkably short lifespans from germination to harvest, but you can't just plant them and hope for the best. Trim them, prune them, feed them, water them, pamper them, and make sure they're getting enough light, CO_2, and ventilation.

Don't panic. Most of the problems that occur with plants are the result of easily reversible mistakes. For instance, if some of the leaves start to turn yellow and the plant starts to wilt, it could just be lacking in one particular nutrient. Some leaves on the plant will also just die either because of a lack of light or because of natural processes. In general, it's not indicative of a greater problem throughout the plant.

No matter what happens, don't be afraid. Do not panic if your plant starts to wilt or turn yellow for example. A lot of these symptoms are easily reversible and may just need a slight adjustment in nutrients or lighting.

Growing Indoors

Indoor grown weed is at least 15 times cheaper than what is sold on the market. Over a 3.5 month growth cycle you will pay approximately $90 in electricity bills and will yields around 4.5 ounces of dry bud. That's around $20 per ounce.

An advantage of growing weed indoors over growing it outdoors is that it's much more private than letting it grow outside. You also get to have more control over the growth of your weed. However, you'll need a lot of equipment to have things going and you need to make sure that the conditions are optimal for your marijuana plants, especially light since growing indoors robs you of much sunlight.

Growing Space

Every part of the grow space is important to the health of your plants. Setting up a grow room is something that is incredibly important the first time that you do it. Before you can set up a grow room you are going to have to pick the space and understand what you will do with it. Garages, attics, and closets can be great places to set up your grow if you have the room, so think about them before you start trying to do anything more complicated. Primarily, your room and space will have to have an adequate source of electricity and a way to get water into it. Ideally, the room that you are using should also have floors that are covered in either wood, tile, or cement. If you choose to set up your grow room in a space that has carpet, you'll constantly be battling against moisture and the mold and fungus that comes with it. Finally, you'll have to think about windows. Too many windows can give a look into your grow room, which can be a problem. Insulating them in particular will help you keep some of your privacy.

Grow Box

Alternatively, I would recommend you consider a grow box instead. These are tents made from a strong reflective fabric. The humidity and bright light stays contained inside. They have openings for air and electric cables. You can also get a grow box fully equipped with lights, ventilation and everything. This is the best option that could save you lots of effort and the trouble of planning and doing every single thing yourself.

Do not make the mistake of buying a grow box that is too small. Even smallest setups need at least a height of 62 inches (1.60m). Normal operations are at least 70 inches (1.80m). Because weed grows tall and you also need to calculate that lamp and filter take up space. As for width and depth, it does not really matter. Buy as suitable for your space.

Growing Medium

A grow medium is the substance you decide to grow your cannabis plants in. Each type has its advantages and disadvantages, affecting how you plants will grow. You will find that a variety of cultivators of varying skill levels all have their own personal favorites and it will come down to time and experience for you to work out what is best for you. Growing mediums fall into one of two categories, either soil based growth mediums that usually contain a natural organic nutrient content - soil; or hydroponic based growth mediums, such as clay pellets or rockwool - these usually have no nutritional content.

Soil

Soil based mediums are the most commonly used form of growing medium. This is because they are cheap, easy to manage and fairly straightforward to maintain. However, if your soil is not tailored for the growth of cannabis, then no matter how advanced your skills are, your cannabis plants are not going to reach their full potential. As you gain experience knowledge you will begin to gain a better understanding of what your plant needs and create a soil composition that is well suited to your cannabis. When you use a soil based medium your cannabis will grow long winding roots. These roots search through the soil and absorb water and nutrients from it. The soil will also go through drier periods that will allow for air circulation, this gives the roots an opportunity to breath and perform essential respiration. When using soil based mediums, you will want to pay attention to its pH level. pH is a measure of acidity, ranging from 1-14, with 1 being very acidic, 7 being neutral and 14 being very alkaline. Cannabis needs a pH level of 7 in order to thrive.

Soil already has lots of nutrients naturally, since it is made up of organic materials. You will also want to bear in mind the nutrient ratios of bought soil. These are expressed as NPK on the soil packet: nitrogen (N), phosphorous (P) and potassium (K). These are three essential nutrients required by your cannabis plants - and they will be required in different amounts of each. Soil packets will usually express the ratios in the format of 20:20:20. In this example it expresses that the soils is made up of 20% of each nutrient. Different soils will have different ratios.

Potting soil mixes can be found at your local garden center. You do not want a soil that is too light or too dense. Cannabis thrives in a balanced soil that is not to wet (dense) or dry (light). Wet soils will not allow enough oxygen to the roots as it remains water-logged, whereas dry soil drains too quickly, make it hard for the cannabis to obtain any moisture. Soil packets should indicate whether they are a particularly wet or dry soil. Read the labels and aim for a middle ground.

A Word on Hydroponics

Despite the hype surrounding hydroponics, I would not recommend them to an inexperienced grower. They require a sufficient level of expertise. Hydroponics are popular among the more advanced and experienced cultivators. The advanced control it offers allows experienced cultivators to get bigger buds in about ¾ of the time it would take a soil based grow. Generally, hydroponics are used by commercial growers as they are able to produce larger quantities faster, that's the advantage. A single mistake could devastate your crops.

Hydroponic grows are soilless, they usually involve the use of growth mediums that are flooded with a nutritional solution at regular intervals. These mediums do not possess any nutritional value themselves. Also, they do not buffer the nutritional content passed through them, meaning the roots of your cannabis can get all of the nutrients they need fast and efficiently. However, this also means extra care is needed as it is easy to cause root burn through overfeeding. Hydroponic setups costs a lot more money and require a great amount of maintenance and expertise. Again, it is usually not recommended for the novice grower.

Choosing Grow Lights

When it comes to light, marijuana requires a lot of it. The more light your plants get, the more you'll harvest. By that, I mean light intensity, not so much light duration. In nature, Cannabis will grow best when it has direct sunlight. You can never have too much light. The more intense the light you give, the more you will harvest. Most growers limit their choices to one of the following three: fluorescents, incandescents, and HID (high-intensity discharge) lamps. To save yourself some time and money, it's in your best interest to just opt for HID lamps during vegetative and flowering stage. These are sold as Metal Halide (MH) or High Pressure Sodium (HPS) lamps and they are, without question, the best for your marijuana garden. Although they have a higher up-front cost than fluorescent or incandescent lights, their overall value is much greater in the long run. That's because they don't require as much electricity as the other options, they are brighter, and they also last much longer. Even if you're on a budget and you don't want to throw away money up-front, you must factor in the cost of the electricity bill and bulb replacements.

So, when it comes down to it, MH and HPS lamps represent a much better value and a better product overall. The plants will also need an even distribution of light so that growth is congruent. It is possible to hook up a track system that allows the light(s) to be moved, a lot of professional growers use this technique. The plants will receive an optimal amount of light without the need for extra lights here and there. For seedlings a HPS light bulb can be too much so many growers use fluorescent lights during germination. They don't produce a lot of heat and can be lowered to four inches from the top leaves. Reflective material also helps enhance the amount of light that the plants receive. This can be as simple as lining the walls with aluminum foil or just painting the walls of the room a bright white. While mirrors are certainly interesting decorations, they don't reflect as much light as other material. Large indoor gardens (and the light they require) place some heavy burdens on the electrical capacity in certain locations. Personal growers really won't have any problems, because they might only use a few hundred watts per hour which would add, at the most, about $10 to the electric bill. Extensive growers, on the other hand, might be limited by the size of their circuit. For instance, older homes might only have a 15-amp circuit that can't maintain all the excess light that a large garden needs. Read these articles about HPS and fluorescent lights and let me know what kind of lights you use.

Compact Fluorescent Light bulbs (CFLs)

CFL's are cheap, easy to use, for an alright harvest with not too much electricity used.

CFL Grow Lamps are large Energy savers bulbs. They are very easy to use. Just plug into the electrical outlet. Also they do not produce overly much heat. So you won't need as much ventilation. A smaller fan will suffice. (More on ventilation later). CFLs are typically run with a reflector to direct more light to the plants. With CFLs, you will get a smaller harvest than with other lamps. Use them if you want a small, easy setup and if you don't need that much weed. Very small grow setups can use 1 Bulb. It is better to use 2 bulbs together. CFL Lamps come in different colors. 2700 Kelvin (used for flowering) and 6400 K (for growth phase). You ideally use both together for the whole growth period. But consider that for the electricity used by 2 x Marijuana buds grown under CFL are not as big and compact as with other lamps. However, it is still a good harvest for self-consumption.

CFL Quick Facts
• Easy, just plug & play.
• Harvest will be smaller than with other lamps.
• They do not really save electricity. As soon as you use 2 bulbs (= 250Watt), you could also use a 250 HPS light which will yield more.
• Use these if you're on a low budget or if you intend to grow in a small space.
• 6400 Kelvin for growth phase, 2700 K for flowering,
• Run both 2700K and 6400K at the same time.
• Touch at plastic base only. They break easily and have harmful chemicals inside.

LED Grow Lights

You could think of these as a little bit like the new Porsche. It's one of the fastest cars in the world, yet it uses as little petrol as a Toyota Prius. According to Top Gear's Richard Hammond. LED lights do the same. They use less electricity than CFL lamps and produce as much or more than HPS. But only high quality LED lights. There are many LED grow lights sold on eBay with cheap components. They won't perform well. At all.

Genuine CREE LEDs seem to be the best. But, they are often faked. It's important to check the sellers' reputation. They are still expensive, but use very little electricity.

LED Quick Facts
• Good quality ones will outperform HPS.
• Huge harvest for very little electricity.
• Good ones are expensive but cheap ones will not work.
• They have a switch to change light color (growth & flowering).
• Get these if you want the newest and best.

Metal Halide (MH) & High Pressure Sodium (HPS)

High Pressure Sodium or Metal Halide bulbs deliver fantastic light for Cannabis. These are slightly more expensive but deliver a lot more light per Watt. HPS are recommended for beginners. You can use them through the whole plant life. MH can only be used during the vegetative phase. If you want to do a perfect job, you could get an additional MH bulb for vegetation.

HPS Lamps (High Pressure Sodium) are still the most commonly used light for growing Marijuana. They produce much more light per electricity used than CFLs. They are as inexpensive to buy as CFLs. You will get a lot more weed out of your operation than with CFL. The weed nuggets will be bigger and harder. But: HPS will produce lots of heat. **You will need good ventilation** (I will explain how). They may be heavier on your electricity bill. There will be more Marijuana scent. Unless you live alone in the countryside, you'll need a filter. They come in 250 Watt, 400 Watt, 600 Watt and even more. Get the 400 Watt version. They do need a ballast which is included when you buy it. Do yourself a favor and get one with a digital ballast. They use less electricity, produce more light and the bulb lives longer.

HPS Quick Facts
• Gets you more weed per electricity used than CFL lamps
• Can be used for the whole grow cycle. Growth and flowering phase
• Buy an additional MH Bulb for extra growth during vegetative phase
• Choose an electronic ballast, not magnetic
• 400 Watt is recommended for medium sized home grow boxes

Get a 250 Watt for a small setup, 400 Watt for average or 600 or 1000 Watt if you want to go beyond personal stash. I recommend 400 Watt. It produces lots of weed while not overly stretching the electricity bill.

So Which Light Is Best for Me?

If you are on a small budget, or have only little space available, or just want to grow a little weed for yourself: Use CFL Lamps. They are easy to use, inexpensive and produce decent results.

If you have a bit of space available, like a pantry or your garage, you could go for HPS Lamps. They produce big, but you'll need a fan to get rid of the heat and may also need to filter the smell with a carbon filter. Read more about building a grow box, if you like.

If you are settled and have mastered the game of money. Or if you are generally into new and fine things, try Hans LED panels. You'll have a silent grow box that uses little electricity and yet produces big yields.

Setting Up Your Grow Room

Set Up Your Insulation

Once you have a plan in place, start getting the room ready. The first step of this is to insulate the walls and windows, protecting against the moisture, light, and circulation issues that can come up. Mylar is the most common solution for this, and it does the best job of keeping out moisture. For the easiest solution, simply tack it directly onto the walls and keep it as flat as possible to keep things nice and neat. This also serves to help reflect the light back towards your plants, making sure that you save money and make the most of the lighting that you install without having to worry about additional reflection methods.

Install The Lighting

As a general rule, you are going to need 600 watts of lighting for every 6 feet of room that you are growing in. This is of course different if you are using LED lighting. It is very important for you to run the wires in a safe place and ensure that you have plenty of space to move around and give your plants the space they need without causing a fire hazard or a less than ideal method of lighting. Hang the ballasts and everything neatly and make sure that your lights are aimed at your plants, something that should go without saying.

The math involved in figuring out what kind of lighting you are using and how much you should have isn't as complicated as you might think, so take your time.

Install The Intake Fans and Exhaust

If your plants are going to have oxygen and stay cool, you'll have to install a quality exhaust system that will take the air out of the top of the room, circulate it, and reinsert it near the floor. Your intake fan should also be smaller than the output fan, making sure that the air flows in the natural way, with hot air flowing toward the top of the room. Experts recommend that the air circulate about thirty times per hour, and moving horizontally to keep the temperature and humidity as level as possible throughout the entire room.

Something that not everyone has to deal with, but if you live in colder climates you will have to think about installing a heater to make sure that the air is the right temperature. Cold air can be great for keeping plants healthy, but you will also have to make sure that it isn't too cold or else you will run into a completely different set of problems.

As an added part of this, you can start installing CO_2 systems that will add even more carbon dioxide to the grow room and help your plants grow even larger. This is typically something that is saved for more advanced growers, but if you feel up to the task and are willing to go through the extra steps, it is well worth the trouble.

Planting Time!

Now you are finally ready to plant all of your seeds. There is plenty more information available about specifics, but in general you will have to germinate the seeds and then plant them, setting them to 24 hour cycles during the vegetative stage. Once they begin flowering, you will be taking them into a 12 on 12 off cycle that will encourage them to start flowering and growing to the maximum potential. With the right kind of attention paid to your plants you'll have incredible success for harvest after harvest, providing you with huge profits and the money to start moving into more advanced grows once you have outgrown this beginner style setup.

How to Germinate Your Seeds

Once the lights are up, you can begin the process of germination. Germination essentially entails taking the marijuana seed and coercing it to sprout. If you don't provide it with the right environment, then the seed will just remain a seed for the foreseeable future. There are several methods that you can use to germinate your marijuana seeds, and every grower recommends something different. For the most part, the options are limited to either using soil (or other growing medium) or using a wet paper towel.

Just by looking at these options, soil seems like it would be the most natural way of germinating a seed. Indeed, simply place the seed about 3 mm deep into the soil, and then keep the soil moist for about 7 days. This usually has around a 90% success rate in terms of getting seeds to germinate, also depending on seed quality.

The wet paper towel method is relatively simple and requires that you place the seed on a damp paper towel and fold it over the top. In theory, the success rate with this method is around 80 to 90%, but it is more common for breakages to occur during transplanting. The seedling clearly won't be able to thrive in a paper towel, so transplanting is a necessity that should be performed with great care.

Watering Seedlings

During the germination period, avoid inundating the seedling with moisture. The top layer of soil should be kept moist, but even then it's best to only use a few sprays of water from a spray bottle. When the plant actually sprouts, the area near the stem should kept dry. This is because moist conditions around the stem are often conducive to stem rot. At this stage (and really any stage) it's relatively easy to overwater marijuana plants. Using excessive water can cause major issues with the soil and major stress with the plants. As mentioned previously, the soil should not be too wet. Indeed, if you make the soil soggy by overwatering it, the roots will essentially drown as a result of the lack of oxygen. This is particularly true when watering small marijuana seedlings in larger containers. These plants won't need to be watered as much as bigger plants because they won't need to take in as much water.

Unfortunately, it can be hard to tell if you are overwatering the plants, because the symptoms for overwatering and underwatering are exactly the same (i.e. the leaves will droop). Obviously, one way to check is by inspecting the moisture level of the soil. You can do this simply by testing the soil with your hand. If the soil appears to be damp, then holding off on watering your plants is the best recourse. It will still have plenty of water to draw from in the soil if it is still definitively moist. If the soil is dry, then adding more water is certainly advisable. As the plants grow, they will require more and more water to quench their thirst. Keep soil moist but not damp.

Light Cycle and Distance from Plants

At this stage, you will keep your plants under 18 hours of light. For the remaining 6 hours they need total darkness. This will be the light cycle during the entire vegetative period. Get an automatic timer which only costs about $8, set it up, plug it in and forget it until the time to switch to flowering comes.

While the seeds themselves won't need light initially, they will certainly need some light when they produce visible sprouts. Light acts as their sustenance at this period of time and it can affect the plants later on in life if they are deprived of the valuable light they require.

In the beginning, the lights should be somewhat close to the marijuana plants. Put your hand on the level of the young seedlings and move the light down slowly until you start really feeling the warmth on your hand. 20 inches away is good rule of thumb for a safe distance.

Vegetative Stage - Grow Your Plant Big and Strong

Once the seedlings start growing normal marijuana leaves, the plant progresses out of the seedling stage, it enters vegetative growth. From this point on try to keep a sharp eye on the distance between the lights and the top of the plant canopy. The accelerated rate at which the plants tend to grow will cause them to inch closer to the lights almost on a daily basis. So, be sure to place the lights close enough so that they provide adequate light energy, but far enough away that they don't burn the tips of the leaves. If it feels too hot to your hand, it's also too hot for your plants.

The growth rate will increase by leaps and bounds, and more leaves and branches will start to appear over time. The seedlings will also finally start looking like actual marijuana plants. From this point on, the plants will largely live out their lives in vegetative growth. It is important to make sure during this stage that you provide them with all the proper environmental conditions that promote growth and higher yields and potency.

Watering - How Often Do I Water My Plants?

We've already seen essentially how the plants should be watered and how much light they should receive. During vegetative growth, the plants are likely going to become "thirstier" and require more water as they get larger. The same rules still apply when it comes to watering: don't severely overwater and don't severely underwater. Many growers develop patterns for watering their marijuana plants. For instance, you might water one day, skip watering for two days, and then water again. It really all depends on the plants themselves. You need to pay close attention to exactly how dry the soil gets after a few days. If the soil is still moist, then you can probably continue on the same pattern, but, if it dries out significantly before the next scheduled watering, you should increase the rate at which you water the marijuana plants.

Fertilizers - NPK

"NPK" (Nitrogen, Phosphorous, Potassium) are the three major nutrients that you have to understand. The NPK is expressed as ratio on your nutrient package or bottle e.g. 30-15-15. This means that the ingredients are 30% Nitrogen, 15% Phosphorus, 15% Potassium and 40% inert compounds like water. During vegetative growth, the fertilizing solution should be one in which the concentration of N is higher than or equal to both P and K e.g. 30-15-15.

Less is more! In most cases, the plant won't need to be fed that frequently. In fact, you only need to feed it about once every week if everything is progressing satisfactorily. However, you should never feed the plants with 100% of the nutrient content because marijuana plants "burn" easily. Instead, dilute the solution to around 50% so that you don't have to employ a soil flush.

Other important compounds include Calcium (Ca), Magnesium (Mg), and Sulfur (S). In general, you might find it difficult to notice any major changes in the amount of nutrients that the plants take in or don't. In fact, in most cases, the nutrient uptake will constitute the least of your worries. As long as the soil's good and you continue to use the same regimen for your nutrient solutions, you should be all right.

During **flowering**, you should feed a NPK solution in which the P has the highest concentration, e.g. 10-50-60 or 0-5-4.

Miracle-Gro is hands-down the best brand of marijuana formulas out there. *Fox Farms'* products are also good. Do not buy a menagerie of nutrient products from different companies as they may not work well together. Stick with one company and one strain until you get a feel for it and have your grow dialed in. Use a basic NPK ratio formula to see what kind of result you can achieve. Only then should you try a specialty product or try switching manufacturers. Remember that there are no magical, miracle products that will make your plants 'explode' and 'drip with resins'.

Air - Ventilation

As you should remember from school, plants need CO_2 to grow. So does cannabis and thus you must supply fresh air from outside the grow room, so it can grow healthily and strong. Ideally, the air should come from outdoors, but air from another room is fine too. If you lead your used air out of a window, your grow room or grow box will suck in fresh air by itself. All you need to do is open a window slightly. Adequate airflow will also reduce problems like mold and make life harder for any insect pests.

As with most living things, fresh air something extremely valuable. Opening up a window or installing a fan system in the room can help provide your plants with some much-needed fresh air. Of course, if it is particularly cold outside, it's probably not a good idea to keep the window open for too long, even if it's your only means of recycling the air.

Temperature

The temperature of the grow room and the plants is also something that needs to be monitored and regulated. The average temperature for a grow room should be around 75*F. But, cannabis is remarkably adaptive and will produce buds lower or higher temperatures. If the temperature drops to extreme lows or rises to extreme highs then you could be in for a surprise when it comes to the quality of your plants. Although cannabis can survive at temperatures around 50 to 55*F, they will not produce the best, most potent bud when the time comes to flower and harvest. In general, keeping the room at about 75*F is your best bet. In reality, plants will grow slightly better at slightly higher temperatures, but it might be difficult to maintain those higher temperatures. You might also need to counteract the extra heat by watering the plants more to cool down the roots.

Sometimes, lights present a problem when it comes to temperature maintenance. Lights that produce a great deal of heat can give the room a sweltering feel and cause the plants to dry up or burn. If this is a problem, then you might want to install an air- or water-cooled system to alleviate the heat emitted from the lights. If you must, you can even install an air conditioner if it is cost-effective for your grow room. Most houses will keep average temperatures that remain around the ideal, but it's important for you to monitor the temperature to ensure that your plants are being taken care of properly.

Humidity

Humidity is basically a measurement of the water in the air. In general, about 40 to 80% relative humidity (rH) is ideal. This can largely be achievable through the use of fresh air as stated above. Some growers even have an rH meter at their disposal to adequately check for ideal humidity percentages. Unless you're planning on having a rather substantial operation, you can probably just get by with a little fresh air once in a while.

How to Force Flowering

After around a month of grow you can consider switching the light cycle to 12 hours of light and 12 hours of darkness. This depends solely on you and how big do you want your plants to get. After you switch to 12/12 they will gain roughly an additional ⅓ of their current size. Once you change the light cycle, a week in switch to a fertilizer that has Phosphorous (P) as its highest value.

During the 12 hours of darkness the room should be kept completely dark with no interruptions. Light cycle interruption could mess up your crop. Turning off the lights won't always do the trick especially if there are other light sources nearby. If you have windows in the grow room, do your best to block them out especially if the sun comes up before the 12-hour period is over.

Determining the Sex

Around 2 weeks into the flowering stage, your plants should start displaying signs of sex. Meaning that by this time that you should be able to tell which is female and which is male. It's not hard at all.

Males

Male plants should be removed as soon as they are discovered as they could potentially pollinate your buds and destroy your crop. A subtle sign is that male plants should already be growing taller than the female plants. By week 2 in flowering, males start developing pollen sacks (balls). They look like this:

Females

The females start developing white hairs called **pistils** that grow out in a "V" shape. Eventually the entire flower that we refer to as bud will be covered with them.

Rarely, cannabis plants develop both sexes, they become hermaphrodites or "hermies". Hermies should be removed as soon as discovered because they can also pollinate your buds. If it has balls kill it.

Now that you are left with only females let them flower and enjoy the show. You'll notice that they will start to grow larger as the flowering period wears on. They will produce more branches, buds, and flowers, and the plant will start to produce more THC overall. It will start to take on a sort of cone shape that resembles a Christmas tree, and you might even start to smell a distinctive fruity or smoky smell. Their pistils will change from the whitish color to a darker shade (generally brown, red, or orange) and, at that point, they should be ripe for the picking.

Feel free to skip the next chapter "Outdoor growing" and go to "Harvesting, Drying and Curing" located on page 68.

Growing Outdoors

Growing outdoors is great. It is virtually completely free and you don't need any additional equipment. If you live anywhere where growing tomatoes is common - you live in a perfect climate for marijuana! Warm climate is great, but weed can be grown absolutely anywhere in the United States and Europe. In the Northern hemisphere, we plant in late May / early June and we harvest in September / early October, depending on the strain. Outdoor plants can become large and yield huge harvests. A single plant could easily yield a couple of pounds. Five and even ten pound plants are not uncommon either. Outdoor grown bud also provides a better smoke and there is certainly nothing more natural than growing your plants outside.

Security

Even if live in a non-prohibition state, you will want to keep your grow out of the public view. The law is not the only concern. Marijuana thieves are becoming a real serious issue because plants could be worth thousands of dollars. If you live in a residential neighborhood, you might be able to get away with growing your plants in your backyard, but you'll likely need to be rather paranoid about keeping the operation under wraps. If you are growing a stinky strain, you could stink up your whole neighborhood.

If you live in a secluded or you own a lot of land, then it might be a little easier to grow your own smoke on your own property. This is really the ideal way to go about it because you can inspect the plants whenever you want without the fear of being caught, plus you avoid the hassle of having to deal with thieves looking to score your homegrown bud.

If want to grow your bud for free and you feel adventurous, you can do a Guerrilla grow. Guerilla growing refers to growing away from your own property, in a remote location of your property where people seldom roam around. Try to grow off your property, on adjacent property, so that if your plot is found, it will not be traceable back to you. If it is not on your property, nobody has witnessed you there, and there is no physical evidence of your presence (footprints, fingerprints, trails, hair, etc.), then it is virtually impossible to prosecute you for it. Always have a good reason for being in the area and have the necessary items to make your claim believable.

Soil

Regardless of where you're growing outside, a good soil is imperative. But, not every kind of dirt will be ideal for growing your marijuana. It's always a good idea to test the ground soil that you're planning to grow in prior to actually using it. This is to ensure that it won't be too alkaline or acidic when the plants start extending their roots even farther into the ground. If the pH test shifts too far in either direction, then you might want to consider a new location, or infuse the soil with some nutrients and fertilizers. Many growers like to use composted material as a natural fertilizer. Anything that once was organic can be used as compost. This means that you can gather leaves, banana peels, and even dog droppings, and, in a few months, you'll have a nice, nutrient-rich fertilizer. Obviously, you can't just take the leaves or shrubs or banana peels and use them as a fertilizer if they haven't decayed. But, virtually any decayed organic material makes for a cheap fertilizer.

You can also buy other fertilizers from the store. A fertilizer with an NPK ratio of around 5:1:1 (just like before) will be the best option. Any fertilizer that has more nitrogen than the other two nutrients will be ideal for most of the plant's life, up until flowering when more phosphorous is ideal. Of course, if guerrilla farming is your preferred method of growing, then you won't really have these options at your disposal. In fact, unless you have a definitive location picked out months ahead of time, you won't really have the option of creating a more workable soil. You'll just have to go with what you can find, as hiking in your own fertilizer could make it exceedingly obvious that you're growing something out there.

Sowing The Seeds

Many growers like to start out their seeds with rows that are fashioned into the soil. You don't really need to bury the seeds that deep into the soil. In fact, some growers have been known to just scatter their seeds on top of the soil to get them to germinate. This random seeding is called broadcast seeding. Maybe a more effective way to get the plants sown is by using hills or mounds. You essentially sow the seeds on the tops of small mounds in the soil. This certainly gives you the freedom to plant outdoors even when the soil is somewhat wet. This is because the water is naturally going to drain off the mound so that the seed (and, later, the plant) won't be inundated. In either the hill or row option, try to ensure that the seeds have some adequate soil coverage so that they can stay moist.

Most guerilla farmers employ broadcast seeding to limit any suspicion and because it's a lot easier. If you spend hours building the rows or mounds, there is a strong likelihood that someone could happen upon you. It's also rare to see any uniformity in nature. If your plants are ordered in perfect rows or they are all sitting atop a small mound of some kind, then any passersby (whether on the ground or in the air) are probably going to take notice of the anomaly. Scattering the seeds around definitely gives the area a look of complete arbitrariness the way nature might have intended. The plants will blend in with all of the other scattered trees and/or shrubs and won't be easily noticed by anyone else. Unfortunately, broadcast seeding isn't the best way to ensure that your plants will germinate. If you place a layer of soil over your seeds and gently press them down into the soil with your foot, then there's a better chance that the seeds will germinate. Many seeds, however, will never germinate or will just simply die after becoming seedlings if you try to grow in this fashion. That's why using a large amount of seeds for broadcast seeding is crucial so that you are at least guaranteed some growth by the time they start germinating.

Germination

Just like with indoor germination, outdoor seeds require moisture to germinate properly. Adding too much water can be detrimental, but as long as the seeds are relatively encompassed by some slight moisture, they should start to germinate. Of course, this is easier if you built mounds or rows for the seeds to really maintain moisture. Sometimes, the conditions outside are not conducive to germination or the resultant seedling stage. If you live in an area where the temperatures remain relatively low well into spring, then you may need to germinate the seeds indoors. To do this, just follow the instructions laid out in the indoor growing section on germination above. Then you can transplant the seedlings when the weather starts to improve. Again, transplanting to a secluded location on public land is pointless at best and dangerous at worst. There's a strong likelihood that the plants won't survive the transplant because of all the stress they would be under. There is also a strong likelihood that you could be caught, because it would probably take more than one trip to get all of your plants in the right position. The whole germination process is difficult for guerrilla farmers especially if there isn't a reliable source of water nearby. Hiking in your own water could difficult and but the soil will still need to be moist for the seeds to germinate. If you're interested, read more about guerrilla marijuana farming.

Weeding

As your plants start to germinate, it's important to keep the area free from weeds. Avoid using any weed killers like Round-Up that might also affect your marijuana plants. It should be noted that weeds will end up taking a lot of the water and nutrients meant for your plants if you don't stamp them out quickly. But, the best way to get rid of weeds is simply by pulling them by hand. Trying to kill them with any chemicals will only be bad for the plants that you want to grow to be nice and strong. Obviously, before planting in an area, you should pull out any weeds that happen to be there.

More Sun = More Bud

The benefit of being in the great outdoors is that you don't really need to worry about light too much. The sun will provide all the light a plant could need and much more. There is no way to duplicate the sun's intensity and it's just a better light source than anything you could produce artificially.

If you transplant your plants from indoor artificial light to outdoor sunlight, they could be shocked by the intensity. This would certainly not be an ideal way to start your outdoor growing experience as you might see the plants lose vigor and ultimately die. If you sowed the seeds outdoors in the bright sunlight, then your plants will be acclimated to the sun for the rest of their lives. Even so, when transplanting from indoors to outdoors, place the plants in a location that is shaded for part of the day to begin with to ensure that the sun's rays hit them directly but for a shorter period of time. This is assuming that you will leave them in portable pots rather than planting them directly into the ground. As they start to get used to the sun's rays, gradually move them more into the direct sunlight until they are receiving light all day. This process shouldn't take more than 7 or 10 days to get the plants acclimated to the sunlight

Light can also be a problem if there is something blocking it from getting to your plants. For instance, if you live in a cloudy area, the plants might not be receiving enough light from the sun. You may have to bring the plants indoors at night and put them under some lamps so they get a full complement of light for the day. If you are guerrilla farming in a forested area, then your plants might be at risk of having the light blocked out by the taller trees in the area. Although the trees provide security and cover from any potential onlookers, they may also limit the amount of light that your plants receive. It will be difficult to transplant them once they are in the ground so you may just have to deal with the limited amount of light. When planting on the slope of a mountain, make sure that you plant on the south side of the mountain (if you're in the northern hemisphere). This is because the sun will go from east to west, but it will be in the southern half of the sky. If the plants are on the southern slope of the mountain, they will receive the most sunlight possible throughout the day.

Watering

Watering your outdoor plants can be kind of tricky, especially if they are located in a relatively dry and arid place. If your plants aren't close to a hose, then you'll have to devise a plan to get your plants as much water as possible. Obviously, early on, the plants won't need a lot in the way of H2O, but as they enter into vegetative growth and start to get much larger, they will need more water. Large adult plants can consume up to a gallon of water per day. This doesn't mean that you'll have to water the plants with a gallon of water every day because the soil should retain some of the water from previous waterings (or even rains). If your plants are on private land that you have access to, then there is no shortage of unique techniques that you can employ to get water to your plants. For instance, you can fill buckets up with water and transport them with a truck to the grow site. Try to avoid dumping the water on a single plant and inundating it.

Other growers have set up a drip method of watering that acts almost like a squeeze bottle that has a permanent drip. This method allows the growers to avoid having to water the plants every day while also keeping the soil moist on a continuous basis. Although it is gradual by nature, the drip method keeps the plants relatively healthy and doesn't flood them with water. Grow near water source Marijuana loves water. Of course, you might live in an area where cannabis can grow naturally without the use of any extra water on your end. This is ideal for guerrilla farmers who likely won't be able to check on their plants on a daily basis. If you are a guerrilla farmer and you live in an area where the weather is often hot and dry, then you might need to keep a firm watch on the plants. Hiking in your own water will be difficult on a number of levels, and it's better if you can find a nearby lake or stream that can provide water for you naturally. If your plants are under-watered, then it is likely that they will start wilting. Just be aware that plants will naturally start wilting in the summer as a response to the heat of the sun. The best way to check if your plants are getting enough water is to dig about 6 inches into the soil, making sure not to cut any major roots on the way down. If the soil there is still cool and moist, then the plants should be fine. Many soils are adept at maintaining water for long periods of time so that there is essentially a reservoir of water stored up there. If at all possible, you might want to water your plants with a nutrient solution about once every couple of weeks. As long as the nutrient solution has a higher concentration of nitrogen, than phosphorous and potassium, then it will be good for vegetative growth. For flowering, use a solution that is higher in phosphorous than either of the other two nutrients. This should be done during the time at which you water the plants.

Temperature, Weather, and Air

Obviously, temperature is one of the major issues when planting outdoors. There's not a lot you can do to keep your plants warm enough or cool enough to suit their needs if there should be some weather problems. If your plants or still in pots, then you can move them indoors to avoid any excessive cold at night. When the temperature is particularly hot outside, the roots can start to sort of "boil" in the soil. Keeping them cool with extra water will help ensure that the plants don't start to lose vigor. Of course, being outdoors leaves your plants open for a large variety of other weather problems. Wind, rain, and snow (depending on where you live and when you plant) can all be problems that will hurt your plants. For the most part, high winds won't have much effect on healthy cannabis plants. They generally grow firm stalks that won't need any external support to stay standing. Indeed, most high winds will cause some miniature cracks in the plant's stalk, but, if they are healthy, they will heal themselves quite easily. If the plants are suffering from nutrient deficiencies, however, they may have a hard time recuperating.

This is also true if they are top heavy and susceptible to more angled bends of the stalk. In this case, you might think about staking the plants so that they don't experience any irreparable damage. If you know of a storm that is coming, it's best to find your weakest plants and make sure they have some exterior support to mitigate the damage that the storm might do. To do this, simply place a stake about six inches from the base of the plant, and then tie the plant and the stake together with wire twists or string. For guerrilla farmers, it's a good idea to **not** plant your crop on a slope known to experience mud slides. But, not every slope is going to be an obvious mudslide area. A good indication that the area won't be adequate for your plants is if there aren't any other small plants growing in the area. If all you see is sturdy trees or shrubs, then the slope likely does not support small vegetation. This could wipe out your entire crop over the course of a freak summer storm. In terms of the air quality that your plants will experience, there's nothing better than the great outdoors. Your plants will get all the fresh air they need and plenty of CO_2 to stay healthy.

Outdoor Flowering

For the most part, flowering outdoors will require no input from the grower. Most plants will start adjusting to the changes in the daylight hours and begin the flowering process. The days will naturally start to get shorter which will trigger the plants into flowering organically. For some growers, however, this will not be the ideal circumstance. Sometimes you don't want the plants to enter flowering and sometimes you want them to enter it earlier. For instance, if the weather's still nice and you want to eke out all the vegetative growth you can with your plants, then you'll want to delay flowering as long as possible. By that same token, if you know that the weather will soon become exceptionally cold or at least too cold for the plants to survive, then try to make sure that they start flowering sooner than they might have naturally. For growers that have access to their plants, both of these options are possible. If you want to delay the onset of flowering, then it merely takes a little light during the night. You can accomplish this with a high-powered flashlight shining on the plants once every couple of hours or so for about 10 minutes during the night. This will adequately mess with the natural inclination for the plants to start flowering and they will stay in vegetative growth for the time being.

Obviously, if the weather starts to get cold early where you live, try to ensure that your plants start flowering as soon as possible. But, outdoor plants offer certain challenges to this goal. If the light to darkness period isn't yet 12 hours to 12 hours, then you'll need to make that happen on your own. Using a polyethylene sheet will help block out any sunrise or sunset light so that you can get the required 12 hours of darkness. For instance, if you know that your area is going to get exactly 13 hours of sunlight during the day and that sunset is at 7 PM, then place the sheet over the plants at 6 PM and remove it at 6 AM when the sun rises. After doing this for about 1 to 2 weeks, the plants should start to flower and you can begin harvesting. When it comes to manipulating the flowering period, guerrilla farmers are kind of out of luck. They will be at the mercy of the local weather in the area and won't have a lot of say in the matter. Just trust that nature will work its magic and find a way to give you some excellent smoke.

Determining the Sex

Around 2 weeks into the flowering stage, your plants should start displaying signs of sex. Meaning that by this time that you should be able to tell which is female and which is male. It's not hard at all.

Males

Male plants should be removed as soon as they are discovered as they could potentially pollinate your buds and destroy your crop. A subtle sign is that male plants should already be growing taller than the female plants. By week 2 in flowering, males start developing pollen sacks (balls). They look like this:

Females

The females start developing white hairs called **pistils** that grow out in a "V" shape. Eventually the entire flower that we refer to as bud will be covered with them.

Rarely, cannabis plants develop both sexes, they become hermaphrodites or "hermies". Hermies should be removed as soon as discovered because they can also pollinate your buds. If it has balls kill it.

Now that you are left with only females let them flower and enjoy the show. You'll notice that they will start to grow larger as the flowering period wears on. They will produce more branches, buds, and flowers, and the plant will start to produce more THC overall. It will start to take on a sort of cone shape that resembles a Christmas tree, and you might even start to smell a distinctive fruity or smoky smell. Their pistils will change from the whitish color to a darker shade (generally brown, red, or orange) and, at that point, they should be ripe for the picking.

Harvesting, Drying and Curing

Harvesting

When to harvest

Harvesting is the reaping of the bounty, and is the most enjoyable time you will spend with your garden. Indoor and outdoor harvesting are the same. Plants are harvested when the flowers are ripe. Generally, ripeness is defined as when the white pistils start to turn brown, orange, etc. The time of harvest controls the "high" of the buds. If harvested "early" with only a few of the pistils turned color, the buds will have a purer THC content and will have less THC that has turned to CBD. Buds taken later, when fully ripened will normally have these higher CBD levels and may not be what you prefer once you try different samples picked at different times.

All new growth will stop around the fourth or fifth week of blooming. When you notice the decline, don't start to harvest immediately. Wait about a week after the decline starts to really start harvesting your sinsemilla plants. This is when the THC will be at its highest and the smoke will be the most potent. If you leave the plants in to grow more, they might slowly get a bit larger and produce a few extra buds. But, the THC won't be as potent because it will finally start to degrade.

The best way to tell when your bud is ripe and ready is to use a magnifier and take a look at the little THC crystals on the buds. When it's too early they are clear and transparent. Once they start turning amber it is time to chop. Do not harvest too late! Once they are mostly all turning brownish in color, the THC levels are dropping and the flower is past optimum potency.

Harvesting and Trimming

Harvesting weed takes a lot of time to do. Having patience is very important when you choose to trim each plant by hand and not by using an automatic trimmer, which some people say damages THC trichomes and results in lower potency. I happen to disagree with that because if there is a difference it is not noticeable. Also, especially when dealing with an outdoor harvest is next to impossible to finish trimming in an acceptable timeframe.

Now to actually harvesting your bud. If you are growing outdoors, start by removing all large leaves with a pair of scissors. If not, then you can proceed to chopping and you'll remove them afterwards. Start cutting of branches of easy-to-work with sizes. Try to always leave a V shape set of couple of branches that allows you to easily hang them on a string.

Once you chopped down the entire plant start removing the excess leaves off the flowers as they are on the branch, you want to keep them there. This procedure will take some time until go through your entire harvest, depending on its size and strain you grew, some strains are leafier than others.

Drying

Once the buds of the marijuana plant have been trimmed and harvested, they now need to be hung to dry and cure. This is the last step in harvesting marijuana buds and is also an extremely important one.

Do not dry your bud in the sun, it will be ruined. Use a dark, dry and cool area that has plenty of airflow. When using a closet or a small space to hang dry and cure your marijuana buds you need to remember a few things. The darker the room the better. Light is bad for the THC glands when they are drying and curing. Always have air movement, but make sure the buds are not blowing around, don't let the fans hit the hanging buds directly. Put a small intake fan in one corner and put a small exhaust fan on the floor or up high blowing the air out. The average bud takes 5 days to dry. All plants are different in size and density, therefore drying times will vary.

You can feel the buds to see if they are dry. Keep in mind that even though they feel dry, they will regain moisture once they are put into the cure stage. During drying, you always want to make sure the temperature and airflow are perfect as this will help eliminate mold and nasty odors. Keeping light away from the buds while drying will preserve the THC trichomes, keeping potency at a maximum. While your plants are drying, you should be collecting glass jars with lids on them to use for curing the buds.

Storing Properly

Now that your bud is somewhat dry, you can sample it in good conscience. It will still not taste great. That's why after it has been hanging for a week or so it should be be cured. Grab a branch a bend it, if it snaps it's time for curing. Start picking the buds off the plants and place them loosely in jars. When a jar is about 2/3 full, put the lid on loosely. You still want some air to get into your buds to help the natural breakdown of sugars and chlorophyll to continue. Letting the sugars breakdown makes the smoke smoother, and reducing the amount of chlorophyll in the buds is what reduces the rawness that makes any bud taste green.

Every day, for the first week or two, at least once, and twice if you have time, check each jar for mold and mildew by removing each bud from the jars. After you've checked and removed any buds that looked moldy, replace the buds into the jars. Packing them differently than they were before will help them cure more evenly. A few weeks of being in the jars will have cured the buds quite well, but some prefer a longer cure period. The longer you cure your buds, the smoother the smoke will be. You can always test smoke a bud to see if the rest of your harvest is ready, too. Longer cure periods aren't harmful as long as you remember to check for mold several times a week. Keep your crop separate so that you don't run into a disaster with mold.

Thanks for Reading! Let's Keep in Touch!

I hope that my book is really going to help you along your growing journey! I realize that there is still some room for improvement. Hence, I still only charge **just a fraction of the price** that future readers are going to be paying. I invite you to get in touch with me at eliasvanrijn@gmail.com. Please, let me know how do you feel the quality of the book can be improved and in return **I will be personally answering all questions** that might come up. Also, if you provide me enough insight about what sort of information readers like you would like presented, I will be sending to you all of **my future advanced growing books absolutely for free!** Fair play.

Have fun growing!

Made in the USA
Middletown, DE
21 December 2016